Learn to

Sew for your Doll

A Beginner's Guide to Sewing for an 18" Doll

Sherralyn St. Clair

COPYRIGHT

ACKNOWLEDGMENTS

Front and back cover: The brunette doll is Emma from Springfield Dolls.

INTRODUCTION

Before I had even learned to read, my grandmother taught me how to sew. I do not know who taught my grandmother to sew, but I know that my mother's grandmother (my great-grandmother) taught my mother. I also know that my great-grandmother learned from her grandmother. When my daughter was growing up, she did not have a grandmother living nearby, so she had to learn to sew from me. My daughter and I have both taken sewing classes and I still read lots of books on sewing, but it is a family tradition to learn the first steps of sewing at home.

Because of all the sharp and hot equipment that sewing requires, a budding seamstress needs a lot of adult supervision while learning to sew. I am constantly referring to "your grownup" in the instructions. Mothers and grandmothers work great as sewing teachers, but other relatives or friends are also good choices.

If you would like to teach a special child how to sew, this book presents a series of skills in a learning sequence. It gives you a place to start and then builds on the initial skills.

You can also use the book with small groups. I have taught sewing to scout and church groups. I have even taught a quilting unit to a classroom of third graders. A group setting can offer a very pleasant way to learn sewing. Please check my copyright notice to see the ways that you can use this book with groups.

TABLE OF CONTENTS

Getting Started

Before you start sewing, I would like to introduce you to Florabunda.

Florabunda is a small doll that I designed and made. She is my assistant.

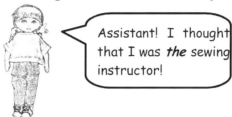

Florabunda is my *assistant* sewing instructor.

She lives in my sewing room and gets into all sorts of trouble.

I mean she is very interested in sewing. She will sometimes explain things or add her opinions to the sewing instructions. Now that you have met Florabunda we can get started.

Equipment You Will Need

Here is a list of the things that you will need as you learn to sew.

Your Grownup

Find an adult who can sew and who understands the sewing machine that you will use. Ask very sweetly for help learning to sew. Be sure to share this book with your grownup.

A Sewing Machine

Foot pedal

It is much easier to sew doll clothes if you use a foot pedal on your machine with controllable speed. A sewing machine that only has a fast speed foot pedal is hard to control while you are sewing short seams and small curves.

Zigzag Stitch

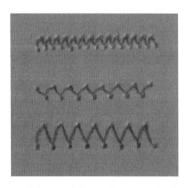

I also suggest that you use a machine with a zigzag stitch. You can use a zigzag stitch for sewing knits. Zigzagging is an easy way to finish seams on doll clothes.

Patchwork Foot

A patchwork foot for your machine is a good thing to have. This foot was made for quilters, but it is great for sewing ¼" (6 mm) seam allowances on doll clothes. When you sew clothes for people, you will use a larger seam allowance and will probably use a different presser foot.

Sewing Basket

Here is a list of sewing gadgets that will make sewing easier and more fun. You can fill a basket or other container with your sewing tools to keep them handy.

Scissors

It is important that your scissors are sharp and well made. Never use your sewing scissors to cut anything except fabric and thread.

Pinking shears are optional, but very good to have. You can use them to finish the seam instead of spending time zigzagging.

Pins and Needles

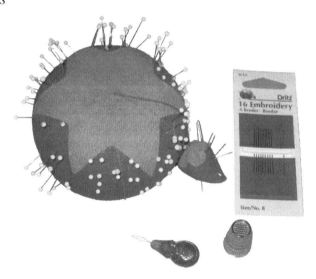

I usually use glass head silk pins, but sometimes I use silk pins with a smaller metal head. Keep your pins in a pin cushion. If they are in a box, they might spill out and stick someone.

I have an assortment of hand sewing needles. Different sewing jobs need different size needles. There are many types of hand sewing needles such as quilting needles, embroidery needles, and needles for upholstery, and dollmaking. The needle I use most often for hand sewing is a size 8 embroidery needle, because it has a large eye that is easy to thread.

Ouch, ouch, ouch. I knew that I should have left my shoes on.

Needle Threader

You will sometimes need a needle threader, even if you can usually thread a needle without it.

Thimble

Not everyone uses a thimble, but I can't get along without one. To use a thimble, hold the needle between your thumb and index finger. Put your thimble on your middle finger and push the needle through the fabric with the thimble.

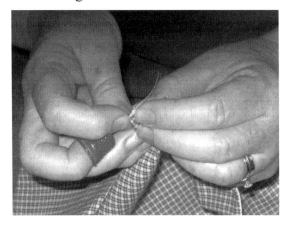

Point Turners

Sometimes we need to sew things together wrong side out and then turn them right side out later. We can use a tool called a point turner to help with this job.

I have two different point turners.

One has a curved side that is helpful when turning curved fabric pieces.

Both turners are helpful for turning corners right side out.

Tape Measure

My tape measure has inches, feet, and yards on one side and metric measurements on the other side. That way I am usually not confused about the two measuring systems.

Help! I'm all tangled up in measurement.

Seam Ripper

A seam ripper is very useful. It lives up to its name by helping sewers rip the threads out of badly sewn seams. I need it more often than I like to admit.

Bodkin

A bodkin makes it easy to insert elastic, ribbon, and string into a casing. I have two sizes of bodkins but I usually use my long bodkin.

Ironing

It is as important to press your sewing project between sewing steps.

Steam iron

Remember that irons can get very hot. Be sure that you have a grownup around to help you use your iron correctly. For our projects in this book we will be using cotton fabric, which uses a hot iron setting. Check the dial on your iron to make sure that you use the correct temperature setting for the fabric that you are pressing.

Spray Bottle

Use a spray water bottle for moistening fabric if you are not using steam in your iron.

Full size ironing board

Set the ironing board to a comfortable height for you to use.

Cutting table

You need a place to spread your fabric and patterns while you are cutting out your projects.

Ironing board

An ironing board with the iron put away usually works for a doll clothes cutting table. I used my ironing board as a cutting table for most of the projects in this book. I found that it is very important to wipe off the ironing board after cutting fabric on it. Otherwise you may find stray threads stuck to the next thing that you iron.

Kitchen Table or Counter

You might use a kitchen counter or table to cut out your projects. Be sure to clean them carefully before and after you use them.

Floor

You can even use the floor as a place to cut out your patterns if your family pet agrees. Many cats and dogs think that fabric and patterns make nice toys or beds.

Craft Table

If you are lucky, your grownup will have a craft table that you can borrow. This table works best of all for cutting.

Doll

You will also need an 18" (45 cm) doll to model your creations. I used Springfield's Emma and a doll that I purchased from our local supermarket while I was designing the outfits in this book. The Springfield dolls can be purchased in craft stores in the US, Canada, and Europe. They can be ordered on line, too. I have also tried the outfits on my American Girl doll and other dolls of this size. These patterns fit most 18" (45 cm) dolls.

Did you see the picture of my new dolls on the book's cover? I'm so proud of them. They're huge!

Making a Bookmark

Here is an easy project to introduce you to your sewing machine. You can turn a piece of light card into a bookmark and learn to work a sewing machine at the same time.

You Will Learn

- How to start and stop the machine
- The difference between a stitch and a seam
- How to guide the stitching to make a straight seam
- How to sew a zigzag seam

You Will Need

- Small index cards
- Colorful thread for your machine
- 100/16 (jean) machine needle (Save this needle for other paper projects after you use it. It will probably become too dull for sewing fabric.)
- Fabric glue or glue stick
- Optional ribbon
- Optional colored pens and pencils to decorate your bookmark
- Optional hole punch
- Optional fusible webbing for a cloth covered bookmark
- Your sewing machine

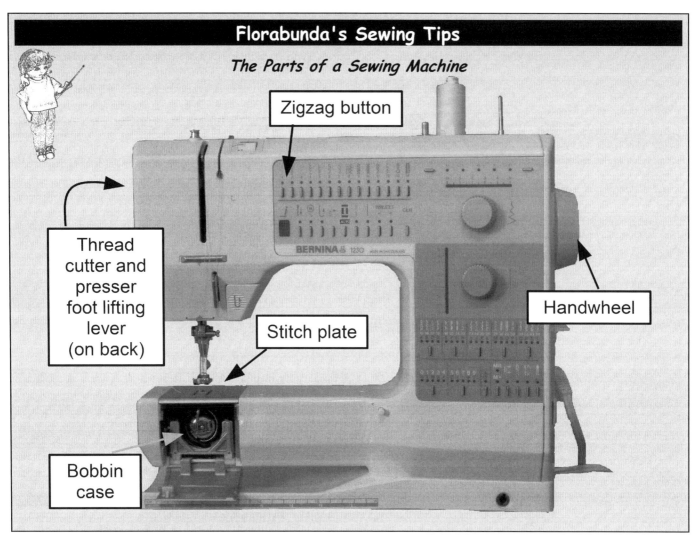

Florabunda's Sewing Tips

The Parts of a Sewing Machine

Zigzag button

Thread cutter and presser foot lifting lever (on back)

Stitch plate

Handwheel

Bobbin case

Parts of a Sewing Machine

You need to know these parts of your sewing machine to follow the directions for making a bookmark. Look at Florabunda's Sewing Tip above. Your machine may look a little different so check in the machine user's guide and ask your grownup for help.

- Foot pedal
- Bobbin
- Handwheel
- Thread cutter
- Presser foot lifting lever
- Needle
- Presser foot
- Stitch plate
- Seam guide

Here are some bobbins. Bodkins make better pointers than bobbins.

On page 14 you can see a picture that shows the needle, presser foot, stitch plate, and seam guide.

I recommend that for your first projects, your grownup have the machine ready for you with the correct needle, thread, and presser foot. Finish a project or two and then your adult can help you learn how to thread the machine, load the bobbin, change the machine needle, and change the presser foot.

I have my spool of thread, my bobbin, needle, and presser foot. Now all I need is a little HELP!

You may want your grownup to demonstrate the steps in this project before you try or you may just want a little help to get started by yourself.

For your first project, you are going to decorate bookmarks with sewing machine stitches.

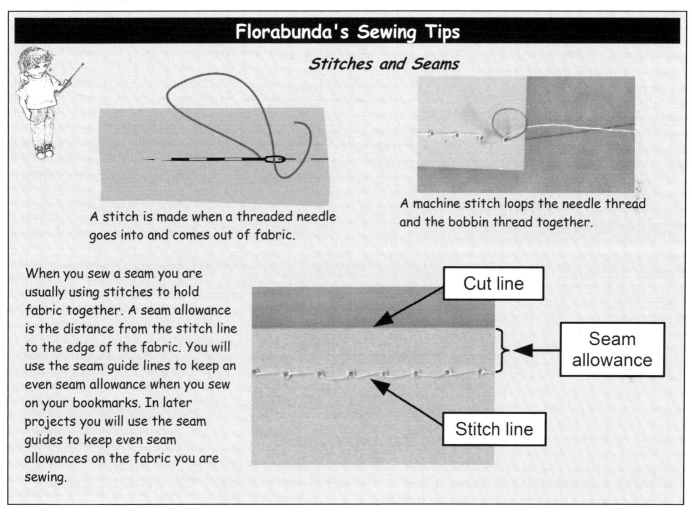

Florabunda's Sewing Tips

Stitches and Seams

A stitch is made when a threaded needle goes into and comes out of fabric.

A machine stitch loops the needle thread and the bobbin thread together.

When you sew a seam you are usually using stitches to hold fabric together. A seam allowance is the distance from the stitch line to the edge of the fabric. You will use the seam guide lines to keep an even seam allowance when you sew on your bookmarks. In later projects you will use the seam guides to keep even seam allowances on the fabric you are sewing.

Cut line

Seam allowance

Stitch line

Making the First Bookmark

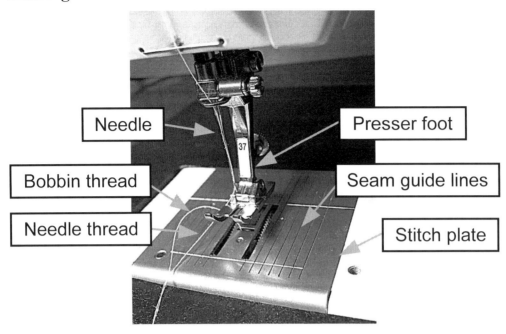

Needle — Presser foot — Bobbin thread — Seam guide lines — Needle thread — Stitch plate

1. Find the ¼" (about 6 mm) seam guide on your machine's stitch plate.

2. Raise the presser foot by using the presser foot lever on the back of the machine.

3. Take your first index card and line up a long side of the card with the ¼" (6 mm) seam guide.

4. Insert the needle into the card by turning the machine handwheel toward you.

5. Lower the presser foot by using the presser foot lever on the back of the machine.

6. Pull the needle and bobbin threads away from you to the back of the presser foot.

7. Hold the two machine threads with your right hand until you have used the foot pedal to sew four or five stitches. If you do not hold the threads during your first few stitches, sometimes the threads get sucked back into the bobbin case. If you are really unlucky, the threads might tangle and the machine will make a sniffing noise like metallic nasal congestion.

Achoo!

8. Guide the card gently with your hands, so that the edge is always against the seam guide.

9. Sew a seam all the way down the card.

10. Raise the presser foot.

11. If the needle is still in the card, raise it by turning the handwheel toward you.

12. Pull the card and threads to the back of the machine and cut the threads with the machine's thread cutter or your scissors.

13. Turn the card ninety degrees and sew across one short side of the card using the same seam allowance.

14. Raise the presser foot and needle.

15. Pull the card and threads to the back of the machine and cut the threads.

16. Turn the card ninety degrees and sew back up the second long side using the same seam allowance.

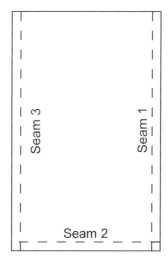

17. Turn your card over so that you can see the bobbin stitches on the back of the card.

18. Pull on the bobbin thread until you see a loop of needle thread on the back of the card.

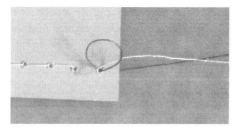

19. Bring the needle thread all the way to the back of the card.

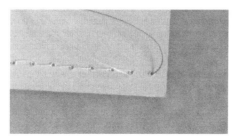

20. Fold the bobbin and needle threads back over the stitching line. Glue threads down on top of a few machine stitches and clip off the unglued parts of the threads.

21. If you wish, you can punch a hole in your bookmark at the top of the card, and thread a ribbon through the hole. Tie a small knot to keep the ribbon on the card.

22. Decorate your bookmark with colored pencils or markers, or leave it plain.

Making More Bookmarks

If your machine makes decorative stitches, you can experiment with them on a new card. My machine can embroider letters, so I embroidered "BOOKMARK" on the card and decorated the edges with a scallop stitch.

If you want to add fabric to a bookmark, you can use fusible webbing. Fusible webbing comes in thin sheets. It is a type of glue that works with your iron. You can iron fusible webbing to a card and then iron fabric onto the card. You will want your grownup to help you if you use fusible webbing.

Before you or your grownup change the machine needle, you should take some time to practice making zigzag stitches on your bookmarks. You may decide to use zigzag stitches to finish the seams of the doll pillowcase and doll clothing that you will make later. The next section will explain finishing edges.

Read the instructions on the fusible webbing carefully, so that you do not glue your card to the bottom of the iron. Take my advice. I know what I'm talking about.

Finishing Edges

The cut edge of the fabric is called the raw edge. Threads can come out or unravel at the raw edge. We finish the raw edges to keep the fabric from unraveling and to make the inside of a sewing project look prettier. Zigzagging is one good method of finishing raw edges. Another good method is cutting the edge with pinking shears.

You can also use a serger, which is a special type of sewing machine, to finish seams. I suggest that you learn to use a sewing machine first. You might learn to use a serger later on.

Making Zigzag Stitches Close to Straight Stitching

After you make this bookmark, you can use the same steps to finish fabric seams.

1. Follow the directions for the first bookmark.

2. After you have sewn straight lines on three sides of the card, go back to the first seam.

3. You are going to make a zigzag stitch next to the straight stitch.

4. Make sure that you are using a presser foot that can make zigzag stitches. I have broken needles when I accidentally tried to use the wrong presser foot for zigzagging.

5. Use the machine manual or your grownup to help you select the zigzag stitch.

6. If you can control the size of your zigzag, set the zigzag stitch about to about ⅛" (3 mm) wide.

7. Make the zigzags close together, but not touching each other.

8. Zigzag close to the straight stitch so that there is about an ⅛" (3 mm) paper edge. If this edge were on a piece of fabric, you would be finishing the raw edge.

9. When you finish the edge of a cloth seam, you should trim the fabric to the edge of the zigzagging. Be careful not to cut any of the zigzag threads. You can leave the paper edge of the bookmark for decoration, however, if you prefer.

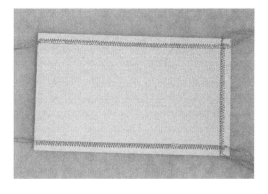

I thought that my bookmark looked prettier untrimmed.

Making Zigzag Stitches Close to the Edge of the Card

After you finish this next bookmark, you can use the same steps to finish single fabric edges in hems and casings. You can also use it to finish the armhole openings on the sundress and summer top.

1. Do not sew straight stitches on this card.

2. Follow the directions 4-7 from "Making Zigzag Stitches Close to Straight Stitching."

3. This time zigzag near the edge of the card.

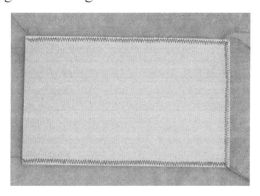

Finishing Raw Edges with Pinking Shears

You can also finish raw edges with pinking shears. Practice using your pinking shears on scraps of fabric.

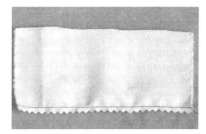

Never cut card or paper with your sewing pinking shears.

When I was sewing the projects in this book I used both zigzagging and pinking to finish the seams. I think that pinking was a little faster, so I used this method more often.

Sewing a Cover for your Doll

Your first project with fabric is to make a cover for your doll to use when she takes a nap.

You Will Learn

- How to find the straight of grain, the cross grain, and the fabric's bias
- How to tear fabric and how to pull a thread and cut fabric
- How to use scissors to cut accurately
- How to find the right and wrong side of the fabric
- How to sew two pieces of fabric together
- How to turn fabric right side out and use a point turner
- How to sew a slip-stitch

You Will Need

- ¾ yd (about 70 cm) each of two different fabrics. One for the top and one for the lining. You will not use all of either piece of fabric, but you should save the scraps to make a matching pillowcase later.
- Matching thread
- Scissors
- Pins
- A tape measure
- A place to cut your fabric
- Your sewing machine
- A hand sewing needle

Find the Fabric's Grains and Bias

Straight of Grain and Selvedge

You want to cut a rectangle with straight sides from the fabric that you picked for the cover top. The first thing the you need to find is the straight of grain.

Look at your fabric. If you have a complete ¾ yd (about 70 cm) piece of fabric, the top and bottom edges will have threads ends sticking out. The two sides will look smoother. The two smooth edges are called selvedges.

The selvedge is where the threads were attached to the loom when the fabric was being woven. The straight of grain goes down the fabric in the same direction as the selvedges.

1. Hold a length of the fabric's selvedge between your hands.
2. Pull gently on the fabric, so that you can feel the fabric being pulled on the straight of grain. Does it feel very stretchy?

Cross Grain

The cross grain runs along the width of the fabric, where you see the ends of the threads sticking out.

1. Hold the fabric with the cross grain between your hands.
2. Gently pull on the cross grain. Can you feel that the cross grain is a little bit more stretchy than the straight of grain?

Bias

1. The bias is slanted from the cross grain to the straight of grain. (It is a diagonal line.)
2. Fold your fabric starting in the middle of the cross grain at the top of you fabric.

3. Make a diagonal fold to the selvedge. The folded part of the cloth should look like a triangle.
4. Gently pull the cloth on the folded line.
5. The fabric should feel very stretchy in this direction. This stretchy part of the cloth is called the bias. The patterns in this book will not be cut on the bias, but it helps to cut you patterns correctly if you understand it.

Cutting the Cover Top and Lining

Cutting or Tearing Fabric on the Cross Grain

You are going to tear you fabric or pull a thread and cut the top of you cover to the right size. Then you will use the cover top as a pattern to cut the cover lining.

Unlike paper, woven fabric has a grain and tearing fabric can give you a straighter line than cutting.

1. Place your tape measure or a ruler on the selvedge at one fabric edge.

2. Measure up about 1" (2.5 cm).

3. Cut through the selvedge at this spot.

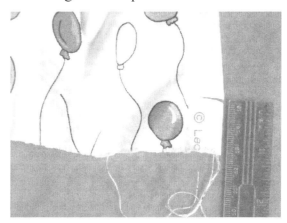

4. Begin at this cut and tear the fabric for a few inches or centimeters.

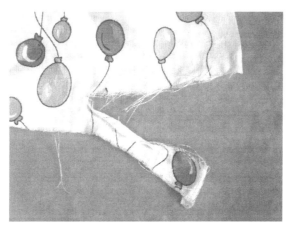

I like tearing fabric because it's so loud.

5. Look at the torn area with your grownup and decide if it is safe to tear across the fabric to the next selvedge. If the fabric does not look damaged on either side of the tear, you can continue tearing.

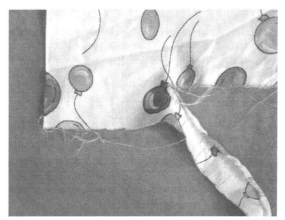

6. If you decide that your fabric should not be torn, then you should pull a thread and cut on the line it makes.

Pulling a Thread and Cutting

If you can't tear the fabric, try this pulling a thread trick. That's a way to get a straight line to follow with your scissors.

1. Clip through the selvedge as you did when tearing the cloth.

2. Take one of the cross grain threads and gently pull it. The thread will probably break before you have pulled it all the way to the second selvedge.

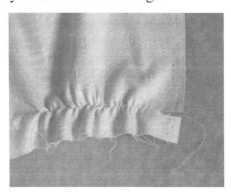

3. Continue pulling the thread after it breaks until you have removed it from the fabric. You should see a faint line in the fabric where the thread has been removed.

4. Cut carefully along this line. Stop cutting at the end of this line and find another cross grain thread to pull.

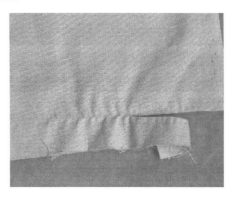

5. Continue pulling a thread and cutting the line until you have reached the other selvedge.

Cutting or Tearing the Second Cross Grain

1. Use your tape measure to measure 20.5" (52 cm) down the selvedge.

2. Clip through the selvedge as you did for the first tear or cut.

3. Tear or pull a thread and cut on the cross grain all the way to the second selvedge.

Tearing or Cutting Down the Straight of Grain to Remove a Selvedge

Usually when you cut out a pattern you do not want to leave the selvedge on the fabric.

1. Look at the selvedge on one side of your fabric. There may be some tiny holes in the fabric along the selvedge. Sometimes the fabric changes color at the selvedge. Sewers usually remove this part of the fabric.

2. Make a clip in your fabric about 1" (2.5 cm) to the right of one of the selvedges.

3. Tear the fabric or pull a thread and cut the fabric all the way down the straight of grain to remove the selvedge.

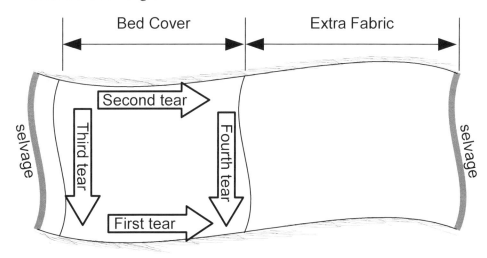

Tearing or Cutting Down the Straight of Grain for the Last Side of the Cover Top

1. Start at the edge where the selvedge has been removed and measure 15" (38 cm) across the cross grain.

2. Clip the fabric at the 15" (38 cm) point.

3. Tear or pull a thread and cut the fabric all the way down the straight of grain.

4. You should have a 20.5" (52 cm) x 15" (38 cm) rectangle to use as a doll's cover top.

5. Press the cover top.

Cutting Out the Cover Lining

You are going to use the cover top as a pattern for the cover lining.

1. To make sure that your lining is straight, I recommend that you tear or pull a thread and cut across the cross grain at the top of your fabric.

2. Find a good spot to cut out your lining. An ironing board will work for later projects in this book, but the cover is a little too wide to cut on some ironing boards.

3. Press your lining fabric and lay it on your cutting table or counter.

4. Lay your cover top on the lining fabric.

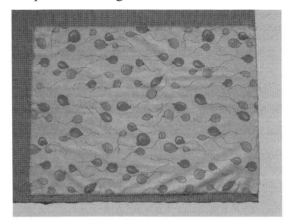

5. The long side (20.5" or 52 cm) of the cover top should be parallel to the lining selvedge. The cover top should be about 1" (2.5 cm) from the selvedge.

6. The short side of the cover (15" or 38 cm) should line up with the cross grain of your lining fabric.

7. Smooth out any wrinkles on the cover top.

8. Use a few pins to pin the cover top to the lining fabric.

9. Cut the lining to match the cover top.

10. To use your scissors correctly, keep as much of the flat edge of the scissors on the cutting table as you can. Try not to lift the fabric up too much as you cut. You want the cut fabric to match the pattern as closely as possible.

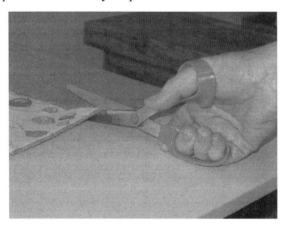

11. If there are any thread "whiskers" on the edges of the cover top left from tearing the fabric, snip them off as you cut the cover lining.

12. Press the cover lining. If the cover top looks a little wrinkled, you can press it again.

Sewing the Cover

Using the Machine

1. Prepare or watch your grownup prepare the machine for this project

    a) Change the needle if you still have the paper sewing needle in your machine. I recommend sizes 70/10 to 80/12 for the fabric projects in this book.

b) Change the thread to a color that matches the fabric that you are using.

c) Use the patchwork presser foot if you have it. Otherwise any foot that will sew a straight seam will work fine.

2. Put the right side of the cover and the right side of the lining together, so that they are touching and the rectangles match.

Florabunda's Sewing Tips

The Right Side and the Wrong Side of Fabric

Much of the fabric that you will use in your sewing projects has a design printed on one side of it. We seamstresses call the side of the fabric with the printing the "Right Side" of the fabric. The side without the printing is called the "Wrong Side".

In sewing directions you will often be told to put the right sides together before sewing.

Some times the directions tell you to put the wrong sides together.

---

3. Use a few pins to pin the two rectangles together.

4. Sew side 1 all the way down the rectangle, the same way that you sewed the index card to make a bookmark. Use a ¼" (6 mm) seam allowance.

5. Turn the cover ninety degrees and sew side 2 using the same seam allowance.

6. Turn the cover ninety degrees again and sew side 3.

7. Remove the pins as you sew to make sure that the needle does not hit any of them. I keep my pin cushion on my sewing machine table and put each pin back in it when I remove it from the fabric. I don't want to take a chance on a pin falling on the floor for someone to step on.

Ouch, ouch, ouch. Not again.

8. Before you sew side 4, start at that side's edge and measure about 6" (15 cm). Mark the spot with a pin. Measure another 3" (7 cm) and mark that spot with another pin. When you sew side 4, do not sew the area between the two pins.

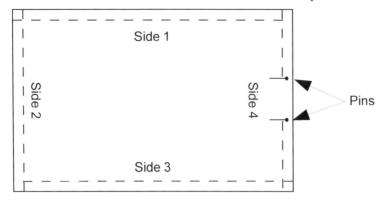

9. When you turn the cover right side out, you want the corners to look pretty. If there is too much fabric at the corners, you will not have clean, sharp corners. To turn the corners correctly, you need to clip them first. Look at the illustration to see where to cut the corners to clip them. Be sure not to cut the threads at the point where the two lines of stitching meet.

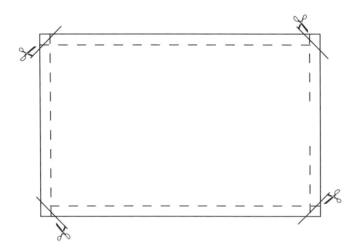

Turning and Pressing

1. Turn the cover right side out through the opening you left in one side of the cover.

2. After you have turned the cover right side out, use a point turner help shape corners. Hold the point turner inside the cover and push gently at each corner of the cover until the corner looks right to you. Do not push too hard, or the point of the turner will push out of the corner and leave a hole in the cover.

3. Tuck in the seam allowances of the turning opening.

4. Press the cover flat.

Hand Sewing the Opening Closed with a Slip-stitch

You need to use a hand sewing stitch called a slip-stitch to close the opening of your doll's cover. A slip-stitch is an almost invisible stitch. You may need your grownup's help with the hand sewing.

26

1. Press the area that you will slip-stitch. For your cover, press ¼" (6 mm) on both sides of the opening to the inside of the cover.

2. Use a few pins to hold the area that you are sewing in place, if you like.

3. Fold an edge back about ⅛" (3 mm).

4. Take a very small stitch through the folded back edge. Pull the thread through the fabric.

5. Catch two or three threads on the other side of the opening and take a small stitch.

6. Take the next stitch in the folded back edge. The stitches should about ¼" (6 mm) apart.

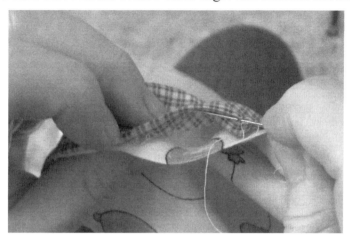

Sewing a Hem with a Slip-stitch

1. The slip-stitch is also a good stitch to use when putting in a hem.

2. Finish the raw edge at the bottom of the skirt or dress.

3. Press about ½" (12 mm) to the inside of the garment.

4. Fold the finished edge back about ⅛" (3 mm).

5. Take a very small stitch through the folded back edge. Pull the thread through the fabric.

6. Take the next stitch on the visible part of the skirt. Catch only three or four threads with this stitch.

7. Go back to the finished edge for the next stitch.

Sewing a Pillow

You Will Learn:

- How to read pattern markings
- How to use a pattern to cut out fabric
- How to mark the fabric correctly
- How to stuff a pillow

You Will Need

- A copy of the pillow pattern at the end of this chapter
- A small piece of cotton fabric (It will be easier to find the straight of grain, if the selvedge is attached.)
- Matching thread
- A small amount of polyester fiber fill for stuffing
- Scissors
- Pins
- A place to cut your fabric
- Washable pen or pencil
- Your sewing machine
- A hand sewing needle

How to Read a Pattern

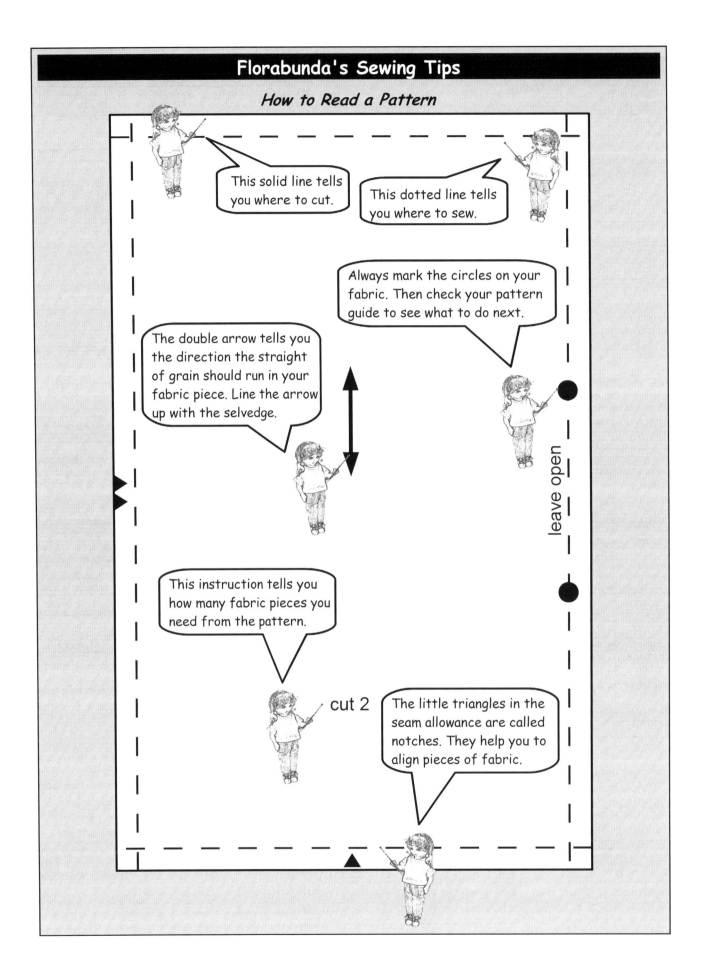

Cutting out the Pillow

1. Copy and cut out the pillow pattern at the end of the chapter. Check your new pattern with the pillow pattern in the book to make sure that it didn't shrink when it was copied.

2. The pattern says to cut 2. If you fold your fabric carefully, you can cut both fabric pieces at once.

3. Look at the double arrow on the pattern. It shows the straight of grain. The arrow should run parallel to (in the same direction as) the selvedge.

4. Fold your fabric on the straight of grain. You do not need to fold it in half. Make sure that there is enough room to fit your pattern so that you can cut both pieces at one time.

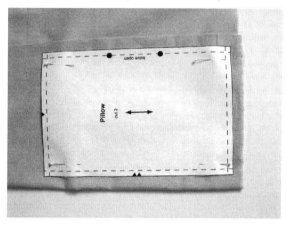

5. Use a few pins to hold the pattern on the fabric.

6. Carefully cut out the fabric to match the pattern.

Marking the Fabric Pieces

Notches

1. Cut out the small notches in the seam allowance that are used to help match fabric pieces.

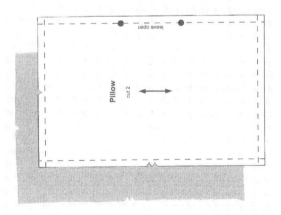

Dots

2. Make a hole in the center of each of the dots on the paper pattern by pulling a pin head through the dots on the paper pattern.

3. Put the pattern on the fabric to be marked.

4. Use a washable pen or pencil to mark the fabric through the holes you made in the pattern.

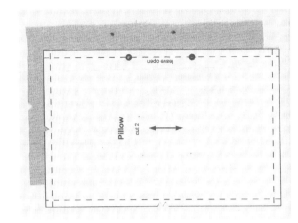

Sewing and Stuffing the Pillow

1. Place the two pillow pieces, right sides together.

2. Sew sides 1-3 of the pillow the same way that you sewed the doll's cover.

See my sewing tip earlier in the book about putting the right sides together.

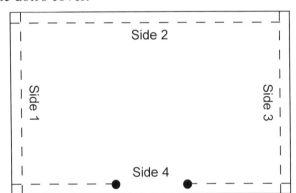

3. Sew the fourth side, but do not sew the area between the dots that you marked on your fabric pieces.

4. Clip corners.

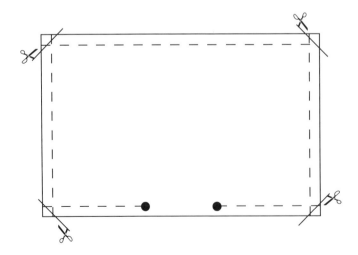

5. Turn the pillow right side out. Use a point turner to help with the corners

6. Stuff.

   a) Use a stuffing tool such as a chopstick to move the stuffing around.

   b) Put some stuffing in each corner of the pillow.

   c) Put in enough stuffing to make your fabric look like a pillow.

   d) Poke it with your fingers to see if it feels soft enough to be a comfortable pillow.

   e) If it feels too hard, take out a little stuffing.

7. Sew the pillow closed with the slip-stitch on page 26.

If you use the pillow before it's closed, it gets fluff all over the bed... Don't ask me how I know this.

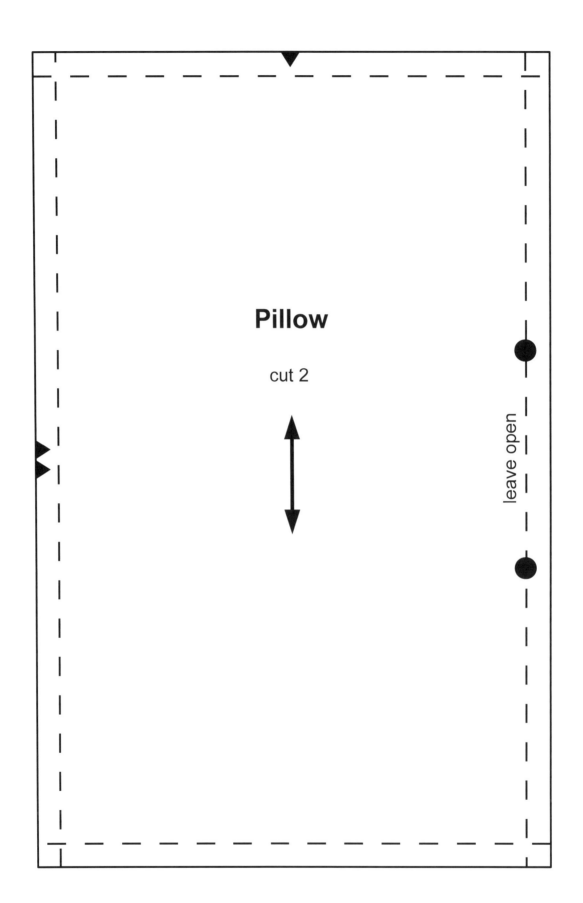

Pillow

cut 2

leave open

Sewing a Two Tone Pillowcase

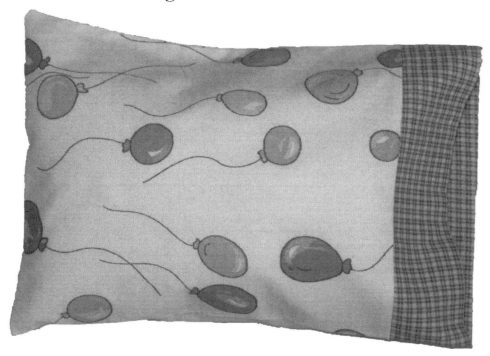

You Will Learn

- How to place and cut patterns on a fold
- How to finish a raw seam

You Will Need

- A copy of the pillowcase and pillowcase trim patterns from the end of this chapter
- The fabric scraps from the top and lining of the doll bed cover
- Matching thread
- Scissors
- Pins
- A place to cut your fabric
- Your sewing machine
- Pinking shears, if you will use them to finish the seam

Cutting and Marking

The pattern says to cut 1 on fold. If the pattern does not have a double arrow, you should fold the fabric on the straight of grain, parallel to the selvedge. Fold your fabric carefully, so that your pattern will fit on the folded fabric.

1. Line up the fold line on the pillowcase pattern with the fold of your fabric. Cut one pillowcase on the fold.

2. Line up the fold line on the pillowcase trim pattern with the fold of your fabric. Cut one pillowcase trim.

3. Mark the notches on the trim and pillowcase.

Sewing the Pillowcase

1. Unfold the pillowcase trim. With the *wrong* sides together fold the pillowcase trim in half long ways. Match the single notches.

This time we are putting the WRONG sides together. See my sewing tip above.

2. Press the trim flat.

3. Unfold the pillowcase.

4. Lay the trim across the right side of the pillow case. Match the single notches. The two raw edges of the trim and the raw edge of the pillowcase should line up.

5. Sew the trim to the pillow case. Finish the raw edges by zigzagging or pinking near the stitching. Review Finishing Edges on page 16 if you need help finishing the raw edge.

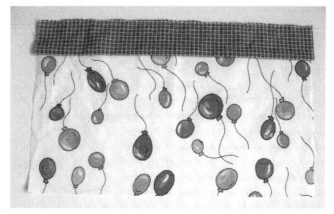

6. Flip the trim to the top of the pillowcase.

7. Press the seam flat.

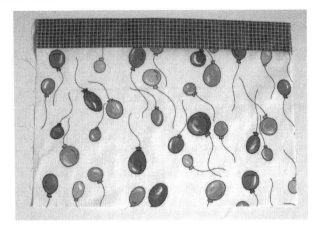

8. Refold the pillowcase with the right sides together. Match the double notches.

9. Sew two sides of the pillowcase. Leave the folded side of the pillowcase trim open.

10. Finish the two side seams.

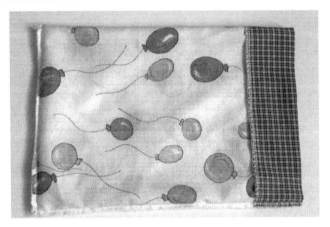

11. Turn the pillow cased right side out and insert the pillow.

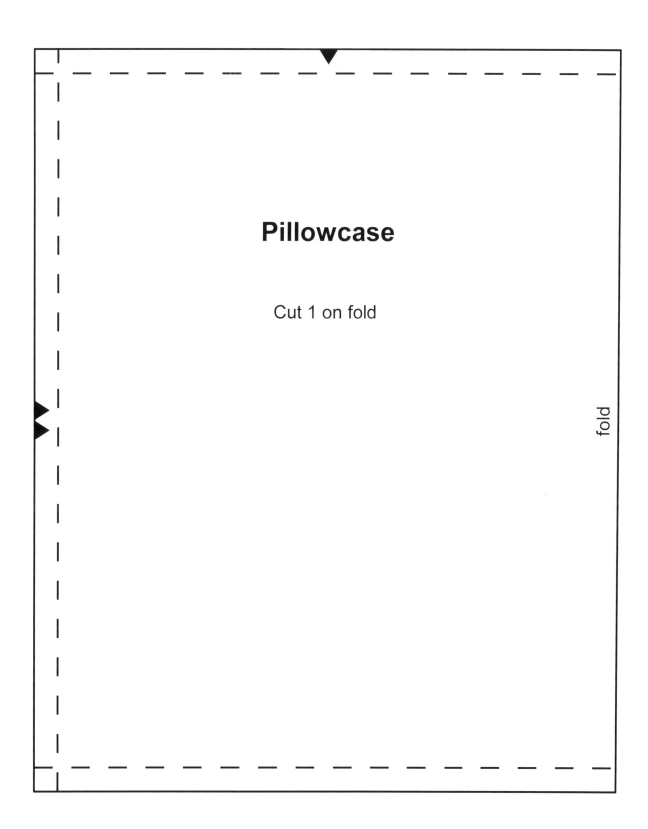

Pillowcase

Cut 1 on fold

fold

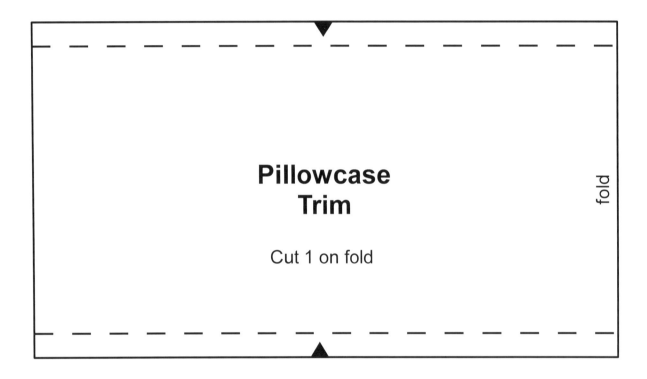

**Pillowcase
Trim**

Cut 1 on fold

fold

Sewing a Simple Sundress and Summer Top

I have a dress just like this. Look on the book's cover.

You Will Learn

- How to gather fabric
- How to topstitch
- How to press a seam allowance to the inside of a garment

You Will Need

- A copy of the sundress and summer top patterns at the end of this chapter
- ⅓ yd (30 cm) piece of cotton fabric in an interesting color or pattern for the sun dress
- ¼ yd (23 cm) piece of cotton fabric for a summer top
- 20" (50 cm) of ⅜" (1 cm) wide ribbon for each dress or top
- Matching thread
- Scissors
- Pins
- A place to cut your fabric
- Washable pen or pencil
- Your sewing machine
- Pinking shears if you plan to use them
- An index card to make an ironing aid
- A hand sewing needle
- A needle threader

Make the sundress first. Then follow the same directions to make a summer top for your doll. She can wear the top with the skirts or shorts that you will make when you get to the next few chapters.

Cutting and Marking

1. Here is how to cut two sundress pieces or summer top pieces on the fold:

   a) Fold your fabric so that you can cut one sundress or top piece on the fold.

   b) Then refold your fabric so that you can cut the second piece on the fold.

2. Mark the notches on the garment's sides and the A dots.

Sewing the Arm Openings

1. Finish the outside edges of the four arm openings by pinking or zigzagging very close to the raw edge.

42

2. Press ⅜" (1 cm) to the inside.

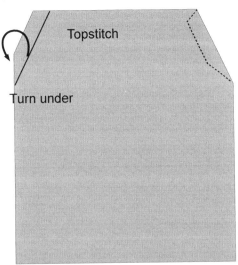

Topstitch

Turn under

Florabunda's Sewing Tips

How to Press a Seam Allowance to the Inside

Cut a ⅜" (1 cm) wide strip from an index card. Pull the edge of fabric over the strip until it just covers the strip. Ask your grownup for help and be very careful with the iron. Press the fabric down so that it covers the strip. Remove the strip and press again.

You can also make pressing strips for ¼" (6 mm) or ½" (12 mm) seam allowances. Sometimes you can find packages of index cards printed with a grid, so that you do not need to measure and draw the lines yourself.

---

3. To topstitch, sew on the right side of the fabric on top of the area that you have just pressed. Use a ¼" (6 mm) seam.

Gathering the Top of the Dress

1. Finish the raw edges at the top of the front and back by zigzagging or pinking very close to the raw edge.

43

2. Press under ⅜" (1 cm) at the top of the front and back.

3. Set your machine to make its longest straight stitch.

4. Pull out about 6" (15 cm) of thread from both the needle and bobbin. You will need to thread a needle with the two lengths of thread when you have finished gathering the dress.

5. Sew a line of long stitches across the top of the dress front using your ¼" (6 mm) seam guide. (Either of your two fabric pieces can be the front. The other piece will be the back.)

6. When you finish the first line of stitches, pull out another 6" (15 cm) length of thread before you cut your sewing threads.

7. Sew a parallel line of stitches using your ⅜" (1 cm) seam guide. Remember to pull out extra thread before and after stitching.

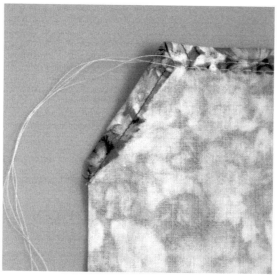

8. Sew the same two stitching lines across the top of the dress back.

9. To gather the threads, gently pull two bobbin threads on each fabric piece.

10. Gather each piece to 4" (10 cm).

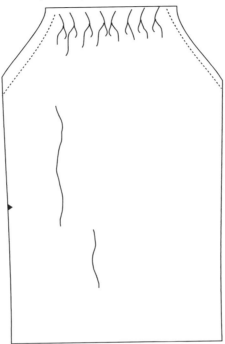

11. Pull all the threads to the wrong side of the fabric as you did with the bookmarks on page 15.

12. Use a needle threader to thread both the needle and bobbin thread from the top row of stitching through the eye of a hand sewing needle.

13. Sew a few stitches in the same spot of the fabric, so that the gathering threads will not pull out.

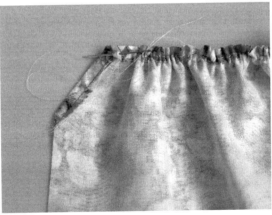

14. Thread the needle with the two threads from the second row of stitching and sew a few stitches to hold this row of gathering threads.

15. Finish hand sewing the gathering threads on both front and back.

Sewing the Side Seams

1. With right sides together, match the notches. Sew the sides together beginning at the bottom of the arm openings.

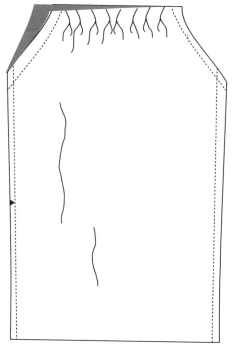

2. Finish the seams with zigzagging or pinking.

Making Shoulder Ties

1. Cut four 5" (12.5 cm) lengths of ribbon.

2. Sew one strip of ribbon at each A dot on the inside of the dress or top.

3. Use a needle and thread.

4. Take five or six stitches in the same spot to hold the ribbons in place.

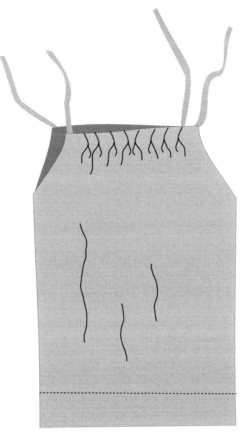

5. When you put the outfit on the doll, tie bows at the left and right shoulders.

Hemming the Garment

1. Finish the raw edge of the hem.

2. Fold and press ½" (12 mm) of fabric to the inside at the hem.

3. Slip-stitch the hem as explained on page 26.

To make a summer top use the shorter summer top pattern. Your doll can wear the summer top with the shorts and skirts that you are going to make.

Hey! I want a summer top, too.

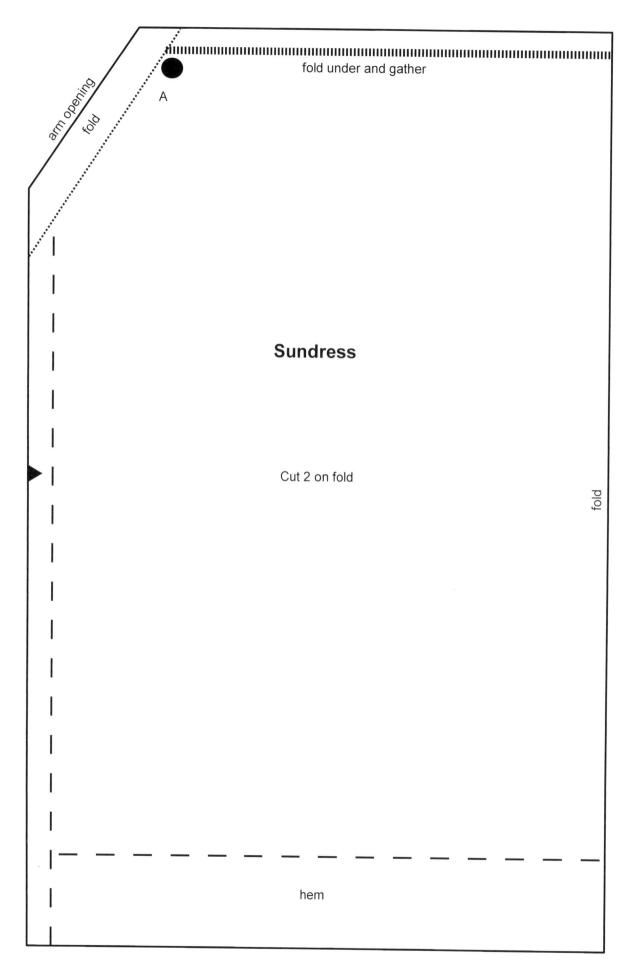

arm opening

fold

fold under and gather

A

Sundress

Cut 2 on fold

fold

hem

48

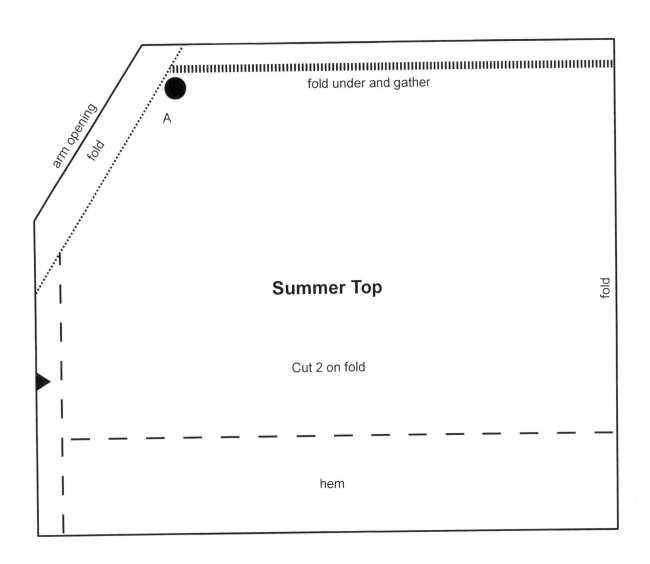

arm opening

fold

fold under and gather

A

Summer Top

Cut 2 on fold

fold

hem

Sewing an A-line Skirt

You Will Learn

- How to make an elastic casing

- How to pull elastic through a casing

- How to topstitch a hem

You Will Need

- A copy of the skirt pattern at the end of this chapter

- ¼ yd (20 cm) piece of cotton fabric in an interesting color or pattern

- Matching thread

- ⅛" (3 mm) wide elastic

- Scissors

- Pins

- A place to cut your fabric

- Your sewing machine

- A bodkin

- Pinking shears, if you plan to use them

Cutting and Marking

1. Cut two fabric pieces from the skirt pattern. One piece will be the front and the other piece will be the back.

2. Mark the notches.

Sewing a Side Seam

1. Sew one side of the skirt front to the skirt back matching the notches.

2. Finish raw edges together using zigzagging or pinking.

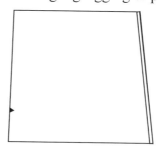

3. Open the skirt out flat.

4. Press the seam so that you can see machine stitching on one side of the seam and pinking or zigzagging on the other side.

Florabunda's Sewing Tips

Casings

A casing is a tube of fabric. We thread drawstrings or elastic through casings to gather the fabric. In a drawstring bag, the casing is gathered around a drawstring to close the top of the bag. In shorts and skirts, the casing is gathered around elastic so that the garment will fit the doll's waist. When it is time to change clothes, the elastic will stretch the waist so that the doll can step out of her skirt or shorts.

Making the Casing

1. To make the casing finish the edge at the top of the waist by zigzagging or pinking very close to the raw edge.

2. Starting at the finished edge, press the fabric ½" (12 mm) to the inside.

3. Topstitch ⅜" (1 cm) from the folded edge at the top of the skirt.

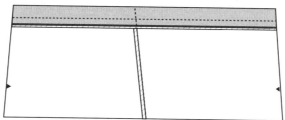

Inserting Elastic

1. To insert elastic into doll clothes I always use ⅛" (3 mm) elastic and my favorite bodkin.

Who in the world has a favorite bodkin?. I like it better as a pointer, but I'll loan it to you to use for this skirt.

2. Pull the elastic into the eye of the bodkin and push the bodkin into the casing.

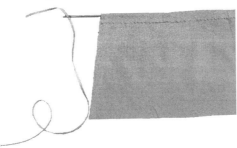

3. Pull the elastic through the casing with the bodkin.

4. Take the elastic out of the bodkin and sew that end of the elastic to the casing. Sew through the elastic several times.

5. Gather the casing fabric over the elastic to about 10" (25 cm). Try not to stretch the elastic while you are gathering the waist.

6. Try the skirt around the doll's waist to check the size.

7. Sew through the second end of the elastic several times.

8. Cut off the extra elastic on both sides of the skirt's waist.

Topstitching the Skirt Hem

1. Finish the raw edge at the bottom of the skirt.

2. Press the hem ½" (12 mm) to the inside and topstitch ⅜" (1 cm) from the bottom of the hem.

Sewing the Second Side Seam

1. Sew the second side of the skirt front to the skirt back, matching the notches.

2. Finish the seam.

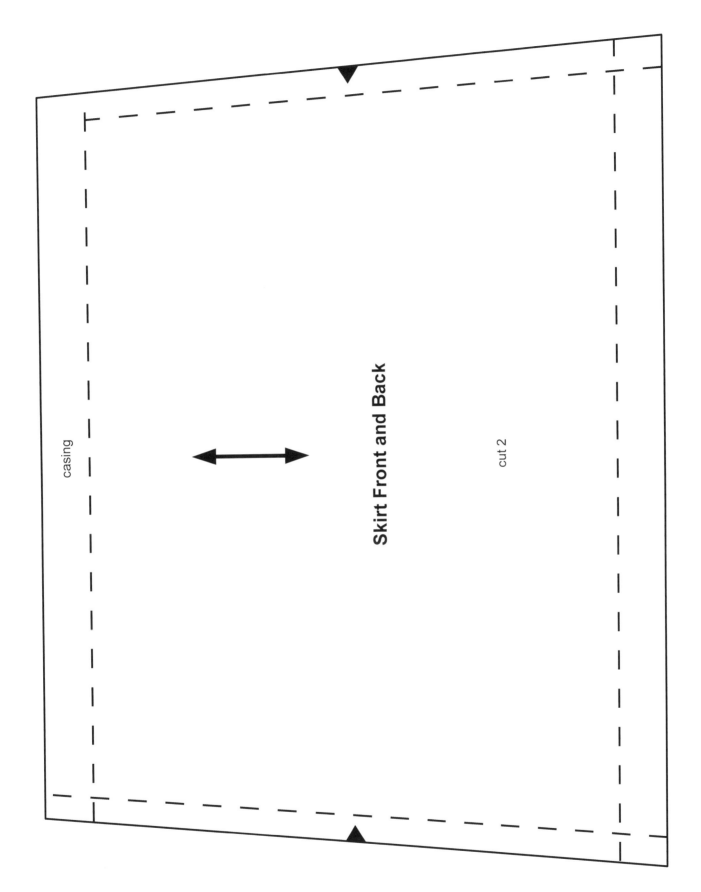

casing

Skirt Front and Back

cut 2

Sewing a Pair of Shorts

You Will Learn

- More about matching notches
- How pants patterns fit together

You Will Need

- A copy of the shorts pattern at the end of this chapter
- ¼ yd (20 cm) piece of cotton fabric in an interesting color or pattern
- Matching thread
- ⅛" (3 mm) elastic
- Scissors
- Pins
- A place to cut your fabric
- Your sewing machine
- A bodkin
- Pinking shears if you plan to use them

Cutting and Marking

- Cut two of the shorts pattern.
- Mark the notches.

Finishing the Shorts Leg Bottoms

1. Finish the legs bottoms on each shorts piece.

2. Turn ⅜" (1 cm) to the inside at each leg bottom.

3. Topstitch ¼" (6 mm) from the edge and press.

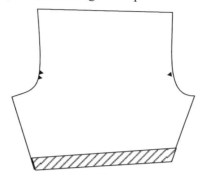

Sewing the Center Front

1. Right sides together, match the single notches and sew the center fronts together.

2. Finish the raw edges using zigzagging or pinking.

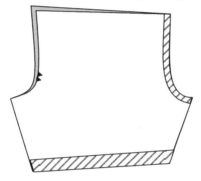

3. Open the shorts out flat.

4. Press the seam so that you can see machine stitching on one side of the seam and pinking or zigzagging on the other side.

Making the Casing and Inserting Elastic

1. To make the casing, finish the edge at the top of the waist by zigzagging or pinking very close to the raw edge.

2. Starting at the finished edge, press ½" (12 mm) of the fabric at the top of the shorts to the inside.

3. Top stitch ⅜" (1 cm) from the folded edge at the top of the shorts.

4. Insert the elastic into the casing. Follow steps 1-8 under "Inserting Elastic" in the instructions for making the A-line skirt on page 52.

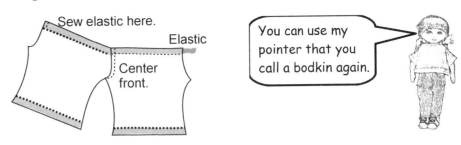

Sewing the Center Back and Legs

1. Match the double notches and sew center backs together.

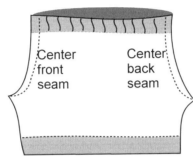

2. Finish the center back seam.

3. Refold the shorts so that the center front is in the front of the shorts and the center back is at the back of the shorts.

4. Pin the legs together and sew the inside leg seams.

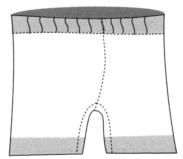

5. Turn right side out.

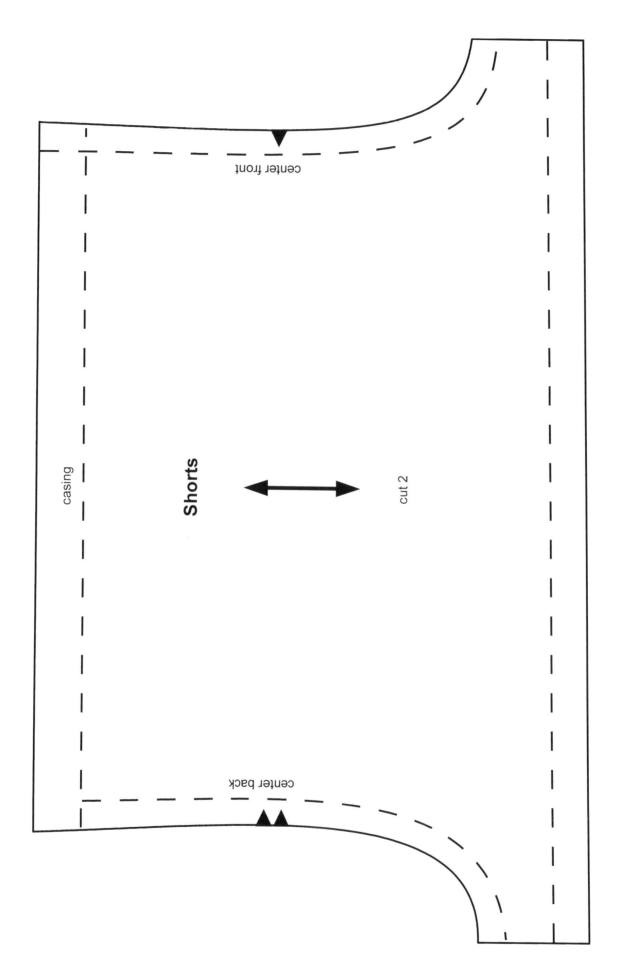

center front

casing

Shorts

cut 2

center back

60

Sewing a Two Tier Skirt

You Will Learn

- To hand baste fabric pieces together before machine stitching
- To sew gathered fabric to flat fabric

You Will Need

- Copies of the two tier skirt pattern pieces at the end of this chapter
- Glue stick or tape to assemble patterns
- ¼ yd (23 cm) of cotton fabric for a single color skirt or fabric scraps for a two-toned skirt
- Matching thread
- ⅛" (3 mm) wide elastic
- Scissors
- Pins
- A place to cut your fabric
- Your sewing machine
- A hand sewing needle
- A bodkin
- Pinking shears if you plan to use them

Gluing the Pattern Pieces

- Copy and cut out the two pattern pieces for the skirt top tier and glue them together.

- Copy and cut out the two pattern pieces for the skirt bottom tier and glue them together.

Cutting and Marking

1. Cut one skirt top tier and one skirt bottom tier on the fold.

2. Mark the notches.

3. Use a pin to mark the center front.

Joining the Gathered Tier to the Top Tier

1. Run two parallel lines of gathering stitches on the skirt bottom tier. Use ¼" (6 mm) and ⅜" (1 cm) seam allowances for the two stitching lines.

2. Pull up the bobbin stitches until the gathered edge of the bottom tier is the same length as the skirt top tier. Match the notches and the center front.

3. Pin and then baste the two tiers.

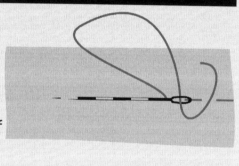

Florabunda's Sewing Tips

How to Hand Baste

Sometimes it is a good idea to baste fabric together by hand-sewing, before sewing the pieces together with the sewing machine. First pin the gathered fabric to the flat fabric. Make sure that the raw edges line up. Spend some time making the gathers even as you pin them. You do not want a lot of bunched up fabric in some spots and two pieces of flat fabric in other spots.

When you are happy with your gathers, sew them together by hand with a running stitch. Make your stitches fairly wide, so that they will be easy to remove when you have sewn the seam on the machine.

4. Machine stitch them together. Use the ¼" (6 mm) seam guide.

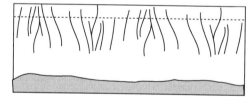

5. Remove the basting threads and all the gathering threads.

6. Finish the seam.

Sewing the Casing and Inserting Elastic

1. To make the casing, finish the edge at the top of the waist by zigzagging or pinking very close to the raw edge.

2. Starting at the finished edge, press the fabric ½" (12 mm) to the inside.

3. Topstitch ⅜" (1 cm) from the edge.

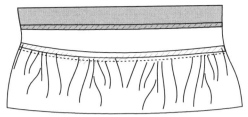

4. Insert the elastic into the casing. Follow steps 1-8 under "Inserting Elastic" in the instructions for making the A-line skirt on page 52.

If you still have my bodkin, you need it again for this.

Finishing the Skirt

1. Sew the skirt's center backs together.

2. Finish the seam.

3. Press the hem ¼" (6 mm) to the inside.

4. Topstitch the hem.

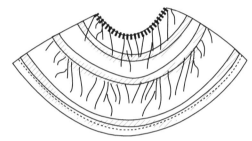

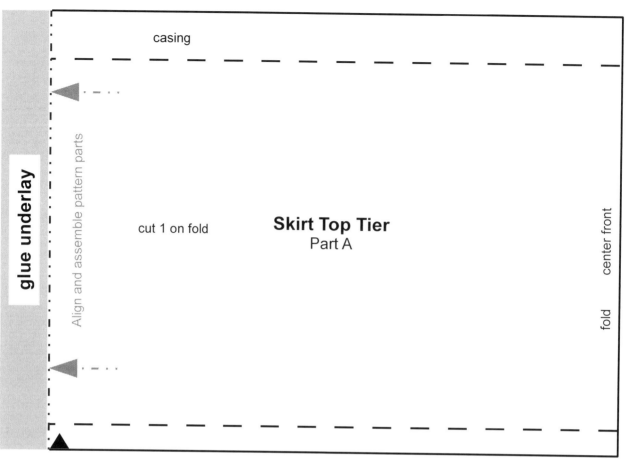

glue underlay

casing

Align and assemble pattern parts

cut 1 on fold

Skirt Top Tier
Part A

center front

fold

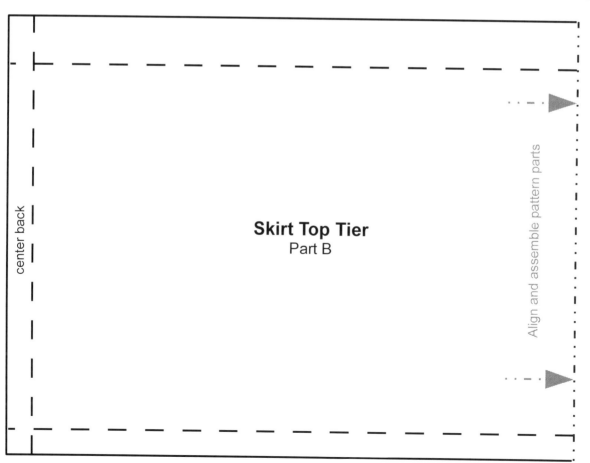

center back

Skirt Top Tier
Part B

Align and assemble pattern parts

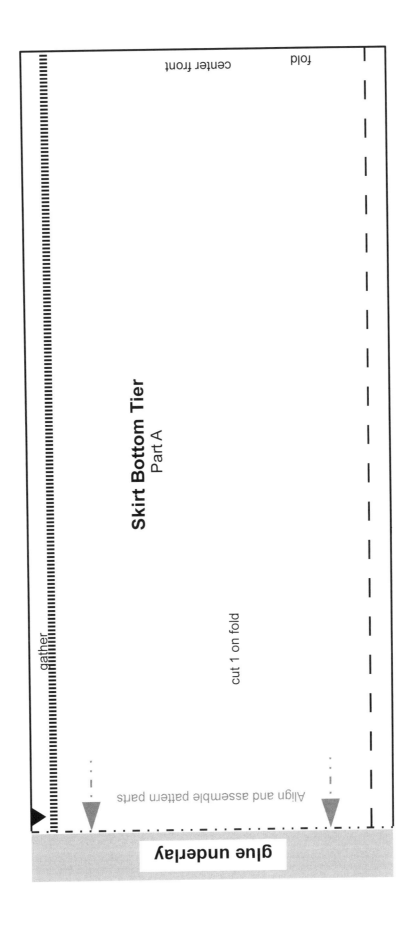

Skirt Bottom Tier
Part A

center front

fold

gather

cut 1 on fold

Align and assemble pattern parts

glue underlay

65

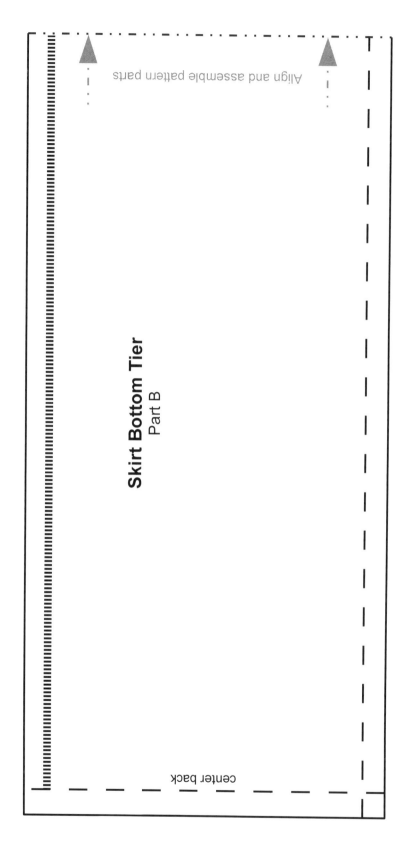

Align and assemble pattern parts

Skirt Bottom Tier
Part B

center back

Sewing a Smock Top and Nightgown

You Will Learn

- How to sew a sleeve that is cut as part of the front and back smock top (not a sewn-in sleeve)
- How to sew a sleeve casing
- How to make a back closing
- How to add hook and loop tape to a back closing

You Will Need

- Copies of the smock pattern pieces at the end of this chapter
- Glue stick or tape to assemble patterns
- Paper (gridded paper is best) for nightgown pattern
- ¼ yd (23 cm) piece of cotton fabric for the smock top
- ½ yard (45 cm) piece of cotton fabric for the nightgown
- Matching thread
- ⅛" (3 mm) elastic
- Matching ribbon for a bow (optional)
- Hook and loop tape such as Velcro®
- Scissors
- Pins
- A place to cut your fabric

- Your sewing machine
- A hand sewing needle and needle threader
- A bodkin
- Pinking shears if you plan to use them

Sew a smock top first. Then cut out a nightgown and follow the same directions to complete it.

Gluing the Pattern Pieces

- Copy and cut out the two pattern pieces for the smock front and glue them together using the directions on the pattern page.
- Copy and cut out the two pattern pieces for the smock back and glue them together using the directions on the pattern page.

- To make the nightgown pattern copy, cut, and glue a second set of front and back smock patterns.
- Glue a paper rectangle to the bottom of each of the second two smock patterns.
- The gown front rectangle should measure 7" (18 cm) by 8" (20 cm) and the gown back should measure 7½" (19 cm) by 8" (20 cm) after they have been glued to the front and back. Cut the rectangles slightly longer than the final measurements so that you will have a tab for gluing.

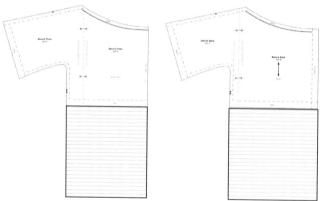

Cutting and Marking

- Cut one smock or gown front on the fold and two smock or gown backs.
- Mark the notches.

Sewing Shoulder/Sleeve Seams

1. Match the single notches at the the shoulder seam/sleeve top.

2. Sew shoulder seams

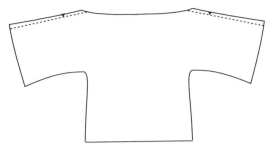

3. Finish each pair of raw edges using zigzagging or pinking.

4. Open the smock or gown out flat and press the seam.

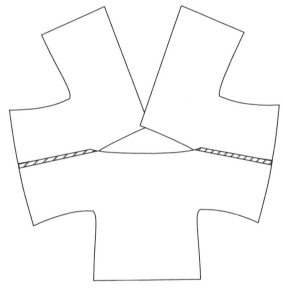

5. Finish the raw edges of sleeves, neck, and back closings by zigzagging or pinking very close to the raw edge.

6. Press the back opening ½" (12 mm) to the inside.

7. Clip about ¼" (6 mm) into the finished edge in of the neck area in the four places shown in the picture.

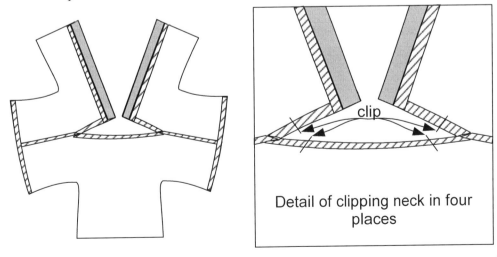

clip

Detail of clipping neck in four places

8. Leave the edges of the back opening folded to the inside and press the neck edge ⅜" (1 cm) to the inside. Always remember to iron safety when you press your sewing project.

Gathering the Neck

You will gather the neck in the same way that you gathered the front and back of the sundress. You can check the instructions on page 43 if you like.

1. Set your machine to make its longest straight stitch.

2. Pull out about 6" (15 cm) of thread from both the needle and bobbin. You will need to thread a needle with the two lengths of thread when you have finished gathering the top or gown.

3. Start at one side of the back opening. Use your ¼" (6 mm) seam guide.

4. Sew a line of long stitches across the neck area to the second back opening. Catch all the fabric layers that have been pressed to the inside of the smock or gown.

5. When you finish the first line of stitches, pull out another 6" (15 cm) length of thread before you cut your sewing threads.

6. Sew a parallel line of stitches using your ⅜" (1 cm) seam guide. Remember to pull out extra thread before and after stitching.

7. Pull the bobbin threads to gather the neck until the neck opening measures 9" (23 cm).

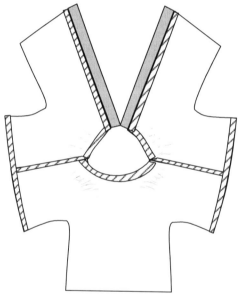

8. Pull all the thread ends to the wrong side of the fabric as you did for the sundress front and back.

9. Start with the ¼" (6 mm) stitch line on one side of the back opening.

10. Use a needle threader to thread both a needle and bobbin thread through the eye of a hand sewing needle.

11. Sew a few stitches in the same spot, so that the gathering will not pull out.

12. Sew the next set of machine and bobbin stitches the same way that you sewed the first set.

13. Sew the remaining two pairs of needle and bobbin threads.

Sewing the Sleeve Casing

1. To make each sleeve casing, press the finished sleeve edge ½" (12 mm) to the inside.

2. Topstitch ⅜" (1 cm) from the edge.

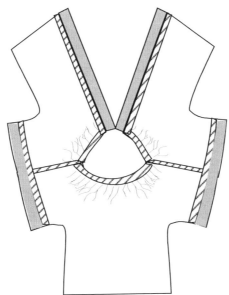

Inserting the Elastic

You will insert the elastic the same way you put elastic in the casings for the skirts and shorts. Check the instructions on page 52 if you like.

This is the last time that I'm going to loan you my bodkin.

1. Pull the elastic into the eye of the bodkin and push the bodkin into the casing.

2. Pull the elastic through the casing with the bodkin.

3. Take the elastic out of the bodkin and sew that end of the elastic to the casing. Sew through the elastic several times.

4. Gather each sleeve to 4½" (11 cm). Try not to stretch the elastic as you gather the sleeve.

5. Check the fit around the wrist of the doll.

6. Sew through the elastic several times.

7. Cut off the extra elastic on both sides of the sleeve casing.

Sides

1. Fold right sides together at the shoulder seams and match the double notches at the smock or gown's sides.

2. Sew across the bottom of each sleeve and down the side.

3. Finish the seams.

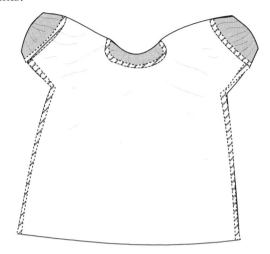

Closing the Back

The gown and smock are closed with short pieces of hook and loop tape. The famous brand of hook and loop tape is Velcro®. If you follow these directions, the left and right sides of the back closing will be side by side, not left side on top of right side like a button and buttonhole closing. You may need your grownup's help for this section.

1. Take a 1" (2.5 cm) length of 1" (2.5 cm) wide hook and loop tape. The hook side and the loop side of the tape should be fastened.

2. Split this tape in half lengthwise so that there are two 1" (2.5 cm) lengths of ½" (12 mm) tape.

3. Separate the tape into the hook and loop sides.

4. Take the hook side of one of the tape pairs and lay it face up partly under the right side of the opening at the top of the opening. About ⅜" (1 cm) of tape should stick out of the opening and about ⅛" (3 mm) of the tape should be under the fabric edge of the opening. The bumpy hook side of the tape should be touching the fabric at this ⅛" (3 mm) overlap.

5. At the edge of the right back opening stitch through the fabric and the tape. You can use a zigzag or straight stitch. I think that zigzagging is a little easier, but I used a straight stitch in the picture.

6. Lay the piece of loop tape completely inside the left side of the back opening. The loops should be out and the smooth side of the tape should be against the fabric.

7. Stitch down the tape through the fabric. A straight stitch looks nicer on this side of the opening.

8. ⅛" (3 mm) from the bottom of the tape, pivot the fabric on the needle and stitch a few horizontal stitches.

9. Pivot the fabric on the needle again and stitch back up the tape.

10. Measure 2" (5 cm) down from the first piece of hook tape on the right side of the opening. Sew the second piece of tape in the same manner as the first tape.

11. Sew the second piece of loop tape to the left side of the opening. Leave 2" (5 cm) between each piece of tape.

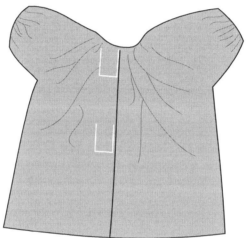

12. Add more hook and loop tape to the back of the gown.

I like to use snag free Velcro®. The snag free variety sticks to itself, so you don't need to worry about hook and loop sides. To use this type of tape, split a single 1" length of tape in half lengthwise so that you have two narrow 1" lengths. Use one piece in place of the hook side and one piece in place of the loop side in the above instructions.

Hem

1. Finish the raw edge at the bottom of the garment.

2. Fold and press ½" (12 mm) of fabric to the inside at hem.

3. Topstitch or slip-stitch the hem.

74

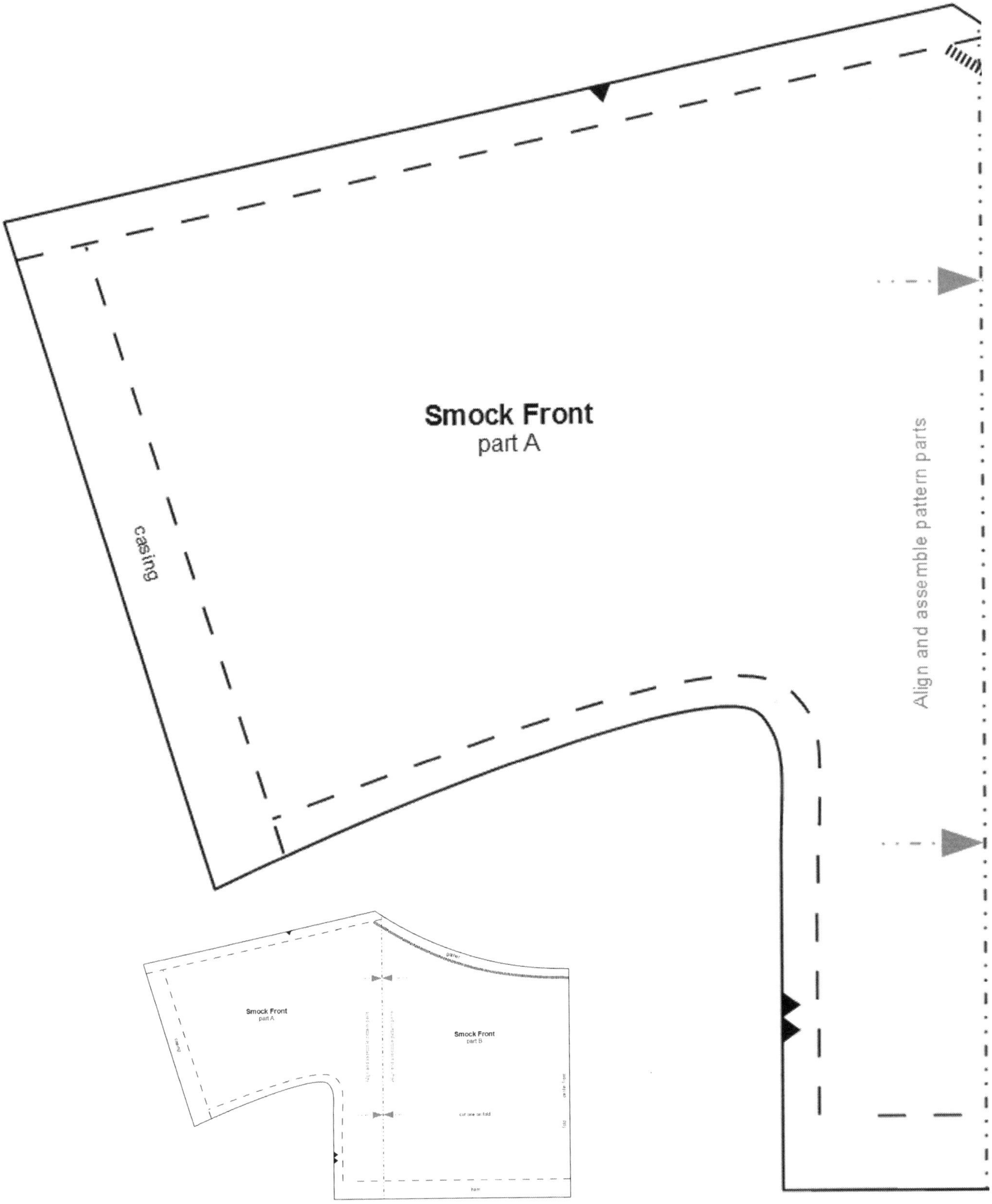

Smock Front
part A

casing

Align and assemble pattern parts

Smock Front
part A

Smock Front
part B

cut one on fold

Parts A and B assembled

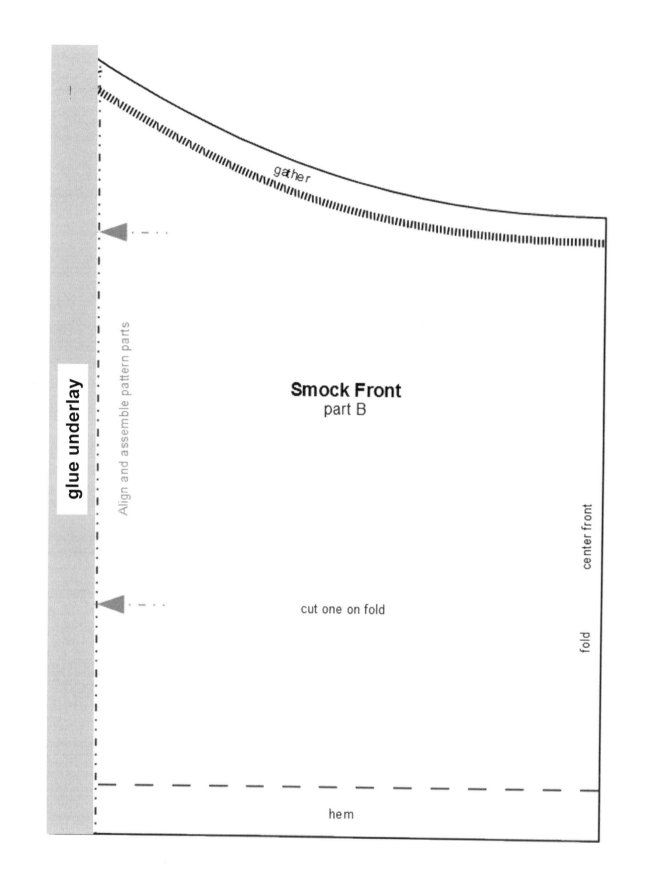

glue underlay

Align and assemble pattern parts

gather

Smock Front
part B

cut one on fold

center front

fold

hem

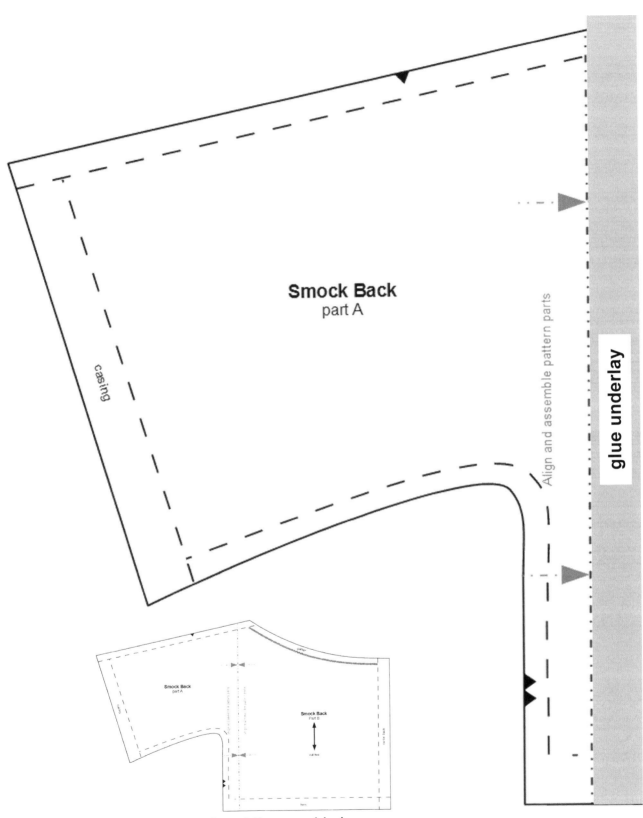

Smock Back
part A

casing

Align and assemble pattern parts

glue underlay

Parts A and B assembled

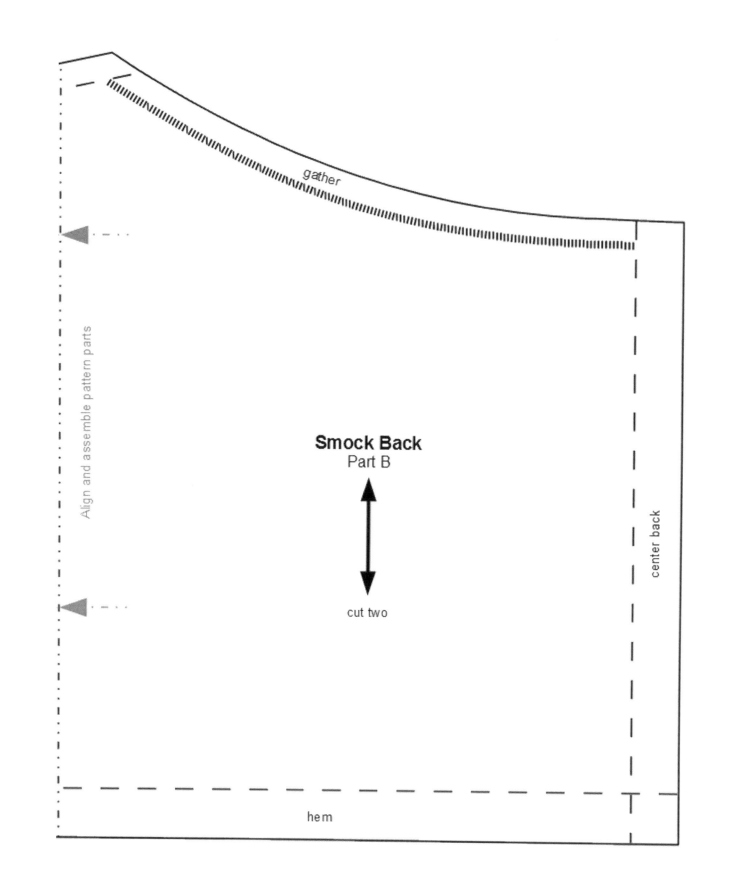

gather

Align and assemble pattern parts

Smock Back
Part B

cut two

center back

hem

78

Made in the USA
San Bernardino, CA
01 July 2014